MY GOVERNMENT

EXECUTIVE BRANCH

by Vincent Alexander

pogo

Ideas for Parents and Teachers

Pogo Books let children practice reading informational text while introducing them to nonfiction features such as headings, labels, sidebars, maps, and diagrams, as well as a table of contents, glossary, and index.

Carefully leveled text with a strong photo match offers early fluent readers the support they need to succeed.

Before Reading

- "Walk" through the book and point out the various nonfiction features. Ask the student what purpose each feature serves.
- Look at the glossary together. Read and discuss the words.

Read the Book

- Have the child read the book independently.
- Invite him or her to list questions that arise from reading.

After Reading

- Discuss the child's questions. Talk about how he or she might find answers to those questions.
- Prompt the child to think more. Ask: Did you know that so many people work in the executive branch of the government? What more do you want to learn about this branch?

Pogo Books are published by Jump!
5357 Penn Avenue South
Minneapolis, MN 55419
www.jumplibrary.com

Library of Congress Cataloging-in-Publication Data

Names: Alexander, Vincent, author.
Title: Executive Branch / by Vincent Alexander.
Description: Pogo Books edition. | Minneapolis, Minnesota: Jump!, Inc., [2018] | Series: My Government
Includes index. Audience: Age 7-10.
Identifiers: LCCN 2017048251 (print)
LCCN 2017058523 (ebook) | ISBN 9781624969300 (ebook)
ISBN 9781624969287 (hardcover : alk. paper)
ISBN 9781624969294 (paperback)
Subjects: LCSH: Presidents—United States—Juvenile literature. | Executive departments—United States—Juvenile literature. | Classification: LCC JK517 (ebook)
LCC JK517 .A53 2019 (print) | DDC 351.73—dc23
LC record available at https://lccn.loc.gov/2017048251

Editor: Kristine Spanier
Book Designer: Leah Sanders

Photo Credits: Evan El-Amin/Shutterstock, cover; H.S. Photos/Alamy, 1; Brooks Kraft/Getty, 3; Getty, 4; Luc Novovitch/Alamy, 5; gradyreese/iStock, 6-7 (background); hocus-focus/iStock, 6-7 (girl); Everett - Art/Shutterstock, 6-7 (portrait); Pool/Getty Images, 8-9; Orhan Cam/Shutterstock, 10-11; Jemal Countess/Getty, 12; 506 Collection/Alamy, 13; Bloomberg/Getty, 14-15, 20-21; Alex Wong/Getty, 16; Alfred Eisenstaedt/Getty, 17; amadeustx/Shutterstock, 18-19; White House Photo/Alamy, 23.

Printed in the United States of America at Corporate Graphics in North Mankato, Minnesota.

TABLE OF CONTENTS

CHAPTER 1
The Top Leader 4

CHAPTER 2
Many Jobs 12

CHAPTER 3
Checks and Balances 16

ACTIVITIES & TOOLS
Take Action! 22
Glossary 23
Index 24
To Learn More 24

CHAPTER 1
THE TOP LEADER

The United States government has three branches. The executive branch, the judicial branch, and the legislative branch. Each branch has a certain job. The executive branch enforces **laws**. The president leads the executive branch.

President Reagan · · · · ▶

The vice president helps, too. U.S. citizens **elect** them both. More than two million people work in this branch!

Vice President Gore

President Clinton

Until 1776, Great Britain controlled the American colonies. Great Britain had a king. But the colonists did not want a king. They wanted a **democracy**. They wanted to be able to **vote** for a president. Who was the first? George Washington.

President
Washington

President Bush

The president is the nation's top leader. He carries out laws. He commands the **armed forces**. The president meets with leaders of other countries. He works to protect our interests. He works to keep peace.

The president works in the White House in Washington, DC. He lives there, too. George Washington is the only president who did not live there. Why? It had not been built yet. It was livable in 1800.

WHAT DO YOU THINK?

The White House has a tennis court. A swimming pool. A movie theater. A bowling lane. Do you think the president should have to live there? Or should the president be free to live anywhere he or she wants?

CHAPTER 2

MANY JOBS

The executive branch has many offices. It has many jobs. Some workers are mapmakers. Some work at the White House. Some answer questions from citizens.

President Obama

The cabinet is in the executive branch. These people advise the president. On what? Many things. The **economy**. Housing. **Security**. Jobs.

What should the president do about an issue? What should he say to other nations? The cabinet helps the president answer questions like these.

The Department of the Treasury is part of the executive branch. One of its duties is to print **currency**. The president chooses the secretary to lead it.

CHAPTER 3

CHECKS AND BALANCES

The president works with other branches of the government. He chooses **justices** for the **Supreme Court**. The Senate must approve each choice. Sometimes the president's pick is voted down. The president must choose someone else.

Supreme Court justices

Congress creates the **bills** that turn into laws. The president signs bills into law. But the president can change bills. Or **veto** what Congress passes. Congress can override a president's veto.

◀······ President Kennedy

The executive branch is powerful. Why? Because the president leads it. But the other branches mean there are **checks and balances**. These stop one branch from becoming too powerful.

Oval Office

WHAT DO YOU THINK?

Should the president have more or less power? Why?

EXECUTIVE BRANCH
enforces laws

power to **impeach**; can override vetoes

can veto bills

appoints judges

can declare presidential acts unconstitutional

LEGISLATIVE BRANCH
writes laws

approves judges

can declare laws unconstitutional

JUDICIAL BRANCH
interprets laws

The president has fun, too. Interesting people visit the White House. The president rolls eggs on the White House lawn every spring. He gets to throw out the first pitch in an important baseball game. Would you like to be president?

DID YOU KNOW?

Anyone who runs for president must be at least 35 years old. He or she must be a natural-born U.S. citizen. And he or she must have lived in the United States for at least 14 years.

President
Trump

ACTIVITIES & TOOLS

TAKE ACTION!

WRITE A LETTER TO THE PRESIDENT

Do you have a question or a concern you think the president should know about? You can write to him! Letters help the president understand how laws impact ordinary citizens.

Write a rough draft of your letter first. Make sure to describe your problem or issue. Be clear. You can also write about your own experiences. If you are writing because you disagree with a decision the president made, make sure you are still polite and respectful. Give reasons why.

The White House requests that letters are written on 8½×11" paper. They can be typed or handwritten. Use ink, and write as neatly as you can.

Address the envelope like this:

The White House
1600 Pennsylvania Avenue NW
Washington, DC 20500

Make sure you stamp the envelope. Then put it in the mail!

GLOSSARY

armed forces: All branches of the military, including the Army, Navy, Air Force, Marine Corps, and Coast Guard.

bills: Written plans for new laws.

checks and balances: A system that ensures one branch of the government is not more powerful than the other branches.

Congress: The lawmaking body of the United States made up of the Senate and the House of Representatives.

currency: The form of money used in a country.

democracy: A form of government in which the people choose their leaders through elections.

economy: The wealth and resources of a country.

elect: To choose someone by voting for him or her.

impeach: To formally charge a public official with misconduct.

justices: The people in charge of the Supreme Court who decide the matters brought to the court.

laws: Rules made and enforced by a government.

security: The state of being free from danger.

Supreme Court: The highest court in the United States.

veto: To stop a bill from becoming a law.

vote: To cast a ballot to make a choice in an election.

INDEX

American colonies 6

armed forces 9

bills 17, 19

cabinet 13

checks and balances 18

citizens 5, 12, 20

Congress 17

currency 15

Department of the Treasury 15

jobs 4, 12, 13

judicial branch 4, 19

laws 4, 9, 17, 19

leaders 9

legislative branch 4, 19

nations 13

override 17, 19

president 4, 6, 9, 10, 13, 15, 16, 17, 18, 19, 20

Senate 16

Supreme Court 16

veto 17, 19

vice president 5

Washington, DC 10

Washington, George 6, 10

White House 10, 12, 20

TO LEARN MORE

Learning more is as easy as 1, 2, 3.

1) Go to www.factsurfer.com

2) Enter "executivebranch" into the search box.

3) Click the "Surf" button to see a list of websites.

With factsurfer, finding more information is just a click away.